WHY FISH
FART

Learn more gross but true facts in

Why You Shouldn't Eat Your Boogers:

Gross but True Things You Don't Want to Know About Your Body

Why Dogs Eat Poop:

Gross but True Things You Never Knew About Animals

WHY FISH FART

Gross but True Things You'll Wish You Didn't Know

Francesca Gould

ILLUSTRATED BY
JP Coovert

G. P. Putnam's Sons

An Imprint of Penguin Group (USA)

G. P. PUTNAM'S SONS
Published by the Penguin Group
Penguin Group (USA) LLC
375 Hudson Street
New York, NY 10014

USA | Canada | UK | Ireland | Australia
New Zealand | India | South Africa | China
penguin.com
A Penguin Random House Company

Library of Congress Cataloging-in-Publication Data
Gould, Francesca, author.
Why fish fart : gross but true things you'll wish you didn't know / Francesca Gould;
illustrated by JP Coovert.—[Abridged edition].
pages cm
Abridged from: Why fish fart. New York : Jeremy P. Tarcher, © 2009.
"Originally published in 2009 by Piatkus as *Horny lizards and headless chickens*."
1. Curiosities and wonders—Juvenile literature. I. Coovert, J. P., illustrator. II. Title.
AG243.G632 2014
031.02—dc23
2013025517

Printed in the United States of America.
ISBN 978-0-399-16598-6
1 3 5 7 9 10 8 6 4 2

Design by Marikka Tamura.
Text set in Diverda Serif Com.

This book is dedicated to
Andrew Bedale
and my gorgeous daughter, Sienna

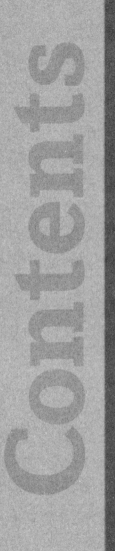

Contents

1 Rude Food 1

2 Disgusting Duties 27

3 Vile Bodies 41

4 They Did What?! 63

5 Weird Creatures 83

6 Deadly Details 117

Coming up...

people
eat live
octopus

1
Rude Food

How Do You Make Bird's Nest Soup?

The Chinese delicacy bird's nest soup is one of those rare dishes that sounds incredibly gross but is in fact far, far worse.

This rare and expensive soup is made from the nests of a certain type of swift that lives in caves in Southeast Asia. The nests themselves are made from the bird's saliva. This saliva sets into solid, cement-like threads that cling to the cave roofs.

the nests are made from the bird's saliva

Collecting the swiftlets' nests from the bat-filled caves is a very ancient and very dangerous job. Nest collectors have to climb extremely high and use long bamboo poles to remove the nests.

To make bird's nest soup, chefs simmer the nests, often in chicken broth, for hours, until they become rubbery. This dish has been highly esteemed since the Ming dynasty, and it is said there is no higher honor one can bestow upon a guest than to serve them bird's nest soup. The soup is prized for its rich nutrient content and supposed health benefits. For centuries, the Chinese have encouraged their children to eat the soup, believing it will boost their immune systems.

Who Eats Tarantula Omelets ?

Despite its frightening appearance, the tarantula spider is regarded as a delicacy by a number of cultures around the world. For example, roasted tarantula is eaten by the Bushmen of central Africa, while people in northern Thailand reportedly like to strip off the spiders' legs and roast the bodies. The Piaroa Indians of Venezuela enjoy eating the big, hairy, bird-eating goliath tarantula (*Theraphosa blondi*), which has a leg span of 10 inches (25 cm), and an abdomen the size of a tennis ball. The whole thing is the size of a dinner plate!

The Piaroa hunt for tarantulas and when they've caught one, they bend its legs backward over its body and tie them together. Next, a leaf is used to twist off the abdomen (to avoid touching the hairs, which can irritate the skin) and the spider is then rolled in a leaf and roasted in hot coals. Once it's cooked, the spider is eaten by picking out the bits of flesh, rather like eating a crab. Apparently, tarantulas taste a bit like shrimp. Bits of the meat can get stuck between your teeth, but luckily the tarantula's long fangs make excellent toothpicks!

Tarantula fangs make excellent toothpicks!

The eating of spiders is also very popular in Cambodia and Laos, where they are commonly toasted on bamboo skewers over a fire and served whole with salt or chilies. Alternatively, some people prefer their spiders fried in butter with a clove of garlic.

What Is Dancing-Eating?

"Dancing-eating," the slang name for *odorigui*, is the Japanese practice of eating live animals. One common odorigui dish is a small, transparent fish called shirouo. More adventurous diners prefer to feast on live octopus. To prepare this dish, the chef will remove the live octopus from a large tank, slice off one tentacle, and then simply serve it on a plate with some soy sauce. Apparently, the limb continues to writhe and twist on your plate, and when you eat it, the suckers attach themselves to the roof of your mouth.

The Japanese are not alone in their taste for very, very fresh meat. In China, there is a popular dish called drunken shrimp, which is also eaten live. When the dish arrives, the shrimp are thrashing around in a bowl of sweet alcohol (with a lid so they won't escape). The shrimp should be left to swim in the alcohol for about five minutes before being eaten. The diner then plucks a shrimp from the bowl with chopsticks, removes the shrimp's head with his or her fingers, and then munches on its twitching body. The Japanese also enjoy a similar dish called drunken crab.

Which Dish, Properly Prepared, Should Contain Just Enough Poison to Numb Your Lips?

The answer to this is the Japanese dish *fugu*, which is also known as puffer fish or blowfish. Fugu is regarded as an exceptional delicacy in Japan, and many say it tastes like chicken, although it is eaten more for the thrill than the taste. Fugu contains one of the most powerful poisons found in nature.

In its natural environment, fugu is a peculiar-looking fish that can puff itself up into a large, round ball when threatened by predators. Besides this, its main form of defense is the lethal poison called tetrodotoxin, which is contained in its internal organs. One blowfish contains enough tetrodotoxin to kill thirty adult humans.

Consequently, fugu chefs need to be exceptionally skilled and precise to ensure that all the poisonous parts of the fish are removed

one blowfish contains enough poison to kill thirty humans

before serving. In Japan, certain restaurants specialize in preparing the fish and removing its deadly poison. If the fish has not been prepared correctly, the toxins can destroy the nerve tissue inside a person's body, paralyzing the muscles necessary to breathe and causing death within about four to six hours. The most poisonous part of the puffer fish is the liver, which should be completely removed during preparation. Apparently, a skilled fugu chef will leave just enough poison to numb your lips. Even so, it's probably best not to annoy the chef.

Why Is Some Coffee Made from Poop?

The world's most expensive coffee is an Indonesian specialty called Kopi Luwak, which is believed to be the best in the world and is very popular in Japan and America. Bizarrely, this coffee is made from beans that have been eaten and then excreted by the common palm civet.

The palm civet is a small, bobcat-like mammal that lives in certain rainforest regions of Indonesia. The palm civet's main diet consists of berries, insects, and other small mammals, but it also enjoys eating coffee beans. However, not just any old coffee beans will do: the fussy civet chooses only the reddest and ripest beans. These beans then pass almost unchanged through the palm civet's digestive system before being pooped out and then harvested by unfortunate plantation workers before being sold

one cup of poop coffee costs over $50.00

for ludicrous sums to wealthy coffee fanatics. Just 2 ounces (57 g) of Kopi Luwak coffee, which is enough to make only one cup, costs over $50.00, making it a very expensive way to start your day!

But what is it that makes Kopi Luwak taste so good? There seem to be two main possibilities. The exceptional flavor may result from the effect of the civet's digestive juices on the coffee beans. Alternatively, these digestive juices may have no real effect, and the answer may simply lie in the civet's fanatical pickiness in selecting only the very ripest, reddest coffee beans.

Which Is the World's Tastiest Insect

For centuries, many cultures around the world have been eating all sorts of insects and bugs. The practice even has a fancy name—entomophagy. In some respects, insects make quite a good meal. They are widely available, easy to cook, and highly nutritious; caterpillars, for example, are chock-full of protein and iron. Bugs that are commonly munched around the world include flies, beetles, dragonflies, grasshoppers, cockroaches, butterflies, moths, mosquitoes, ants, and even bees and wasps. In fact, there are more than 1,900 species of edible insects.

In Nigeria, people enjoy snacking on crickets that are disemboweled and then roasted over open coals. Grasshoppers are also popular, and people working the fields will often eat them raw. In China, a nice warm bowl of earthworm soup is believed to help treat fever. In Macao, you can buy a bag of fried beetles that look like cockroaches. And on the streets of Bangkok, in Thailand, fried grasshoppers are sold in much the same way.

In fact, people in Thailand eat a wide variety of insects, including cicadas, locusts, mantises, deep-fried crickets, grasshoppers (usually fried), dung beetles, moth and butterfly pupae, wasp and bee larvae, termites (in soup), giant water bugs (steamed), bamboo borers (these are small grubs that are sometimes described on menus as "fried little white babies"), weaver ants (which are eaten raw or rubbed with salt, chili, or pepper) and their eggs (these can also be eaten as a paste), and even the revolting-sounding grilled tarantula.

Meanwhile, in South America, tree worms and various stingless bees and wasps are eaten in Brazil. They are apparently known for their pleasant, almondy taste. In Columbia, *hormiga culona*, or "big-bottomed ants," are also enjoyed for their nutty flavor. These winged ants are collected with large sweeping brooms, placed into boiling water, then taken out and dried on the grill. And in the United States, worker ants of this species are sometimes dipped into chocolate.

One company in California makes products such as the Cricket Lick-It, which is a tasty, sugar-free lollipop with, you've guessed it, a real cricket in the center. Perhaps you'd prefer the Scorpion Sucker, which comes in an

Want to try grilled tarantula?

array of colors and flavors—such as blueberry and banana—and contains, predictably enough, a scorpion. If you're not feeling that adventurous, how about a tasty snack of worms? These come in a variety of flavors, including barbecue, cheddar cheese, and Mexican spice.

However, if I had to choose which insect would be the most delicious, I think I might vote for the Australian honey ant. This insect is greatly prized by the Aborigines, who call them by the rather appetizing name *yarrumpa*. This insect stores so much sugary fluid in its body that its hind end swells up into a ball that is big enough to eat. People bite the bug's end off to savor the sweet stuff found inside. They say it's just like eating honey, only crunchier.

Why Did Nelson's Navy Eat Their Biscuits in the Dark?

In the 1700s, under Horatio Nelson's leadership, Britain had the most powerful navy in the world.

However, conditions on board the ships were truly disgusting, and navy discipline was harsh. Floggings were frequent, the pay was low, hygiene was poor, and the food was often infested with bugs.

Before setting off, ships would be loaded with food, including fruit, vegetables, and live animals, but on long trips, eventually there would be a point when all the animals had been slaughtered and the remaining food had rotted. As bread rapidly became moldy, the sailors instead ate "ship's biscuits," also known as hardtack, which were made with flour, water, and salt. These biscuits would often contain weevils or maggots, so the sailors would tap the biscuits on the table to try to knock out most of the bugs before eating. For this reason, many sailors would wait until dark to eat them, so they wouldn't have to see the maggots crawling inside.

many sailors would wait until dark to eat

What Is the King of Fruit?

The durian is a peculiar-looking, disgusting-smelling, melon-like fruit that is nonetheless considered a delicacy by millions of people in the Far East. In Indonesia, Malaysia, and especially Thailand, it is affectionately known as the King of Fruit and, despite its disgusting smell, it is very popular in Southeast Asian markets.

The durian fruit can weigh as much as 10 pounds (4.5 kg) and has a hard green shell studded with spikes. The fruit grows at the top of durian trees, which can reach up to 164 feet (50 m) in height. As if this fruit were not unpleasant enough in its appearance and odor, it also presents a physical danger, as it has been known to drop from the branches and kill people below.

Apparently, the durian tastes like a rich, buttery

smells like a dead rat decomposing in a plate of vomit

custard, highly flavored with almonds. Unfortunately, however, many people find the smell far too off-putting to consider actually tasting the thing. This smell is variously described as being like poop, stale vomit, or even like a dead rat decomposing in a plate of vomit.

Because of the durian fruit's awful smell, the governments of many Asian countries have banned people from taking the fruit onto public transportation. It is also banned by most hotels and airlines in the region, and rental car agencies will reportedly fine you if the car stinks of it when you hand in the keys.

How Do You Make a Fly Burger ?

It takes a lot of flies to make a fly burger, but it might not take as long as you think to catch enough for one.

Lake Victoria in Africa is the second-biggest freshwater lake in the world. At certain times of the year, peculiar dense clouds appear to hover over the lake. These clouds are made up of trillions of lake flies, which make up the largest swarm on Earth. These swarming gnats are called *E sami* by the local people, and the clouds are visible on the horizon from miles away.

When the flies reach land, the air becomes thick with them. Some of the locals hide indoors, but others take advantage of this blight by catching the flies for food. Entire villages will come together to catch the flies in items such as nets, baskets, pots, and frying pans. One popular way of catching the flies is simply to dampen the inside of a pan—the flies stick to it and can then be cooked.

each burger contains about half a million flies

Each village has its own recipe, but one of the most popular and widespread is the fly burger, which is also extremely nutritious. Fly burgers are made by crushing a handful of flies, which are then molded into the shape of a burger and left to dry in the sun. The burger is then cooked—some regions like to roast them, while others enjoy their fly burgers deep-fried. Each burger contains about half a million flies and seven times more protein than a hamburger.

What Is a Cod Worm ?

Have you ever been digging into your fish and chips and noticed a worm inside your fish? If so, it was probably a type of round worm called a cod worm (*Phocanema decipiens*). Cod worms can grow to about 1.5 inches (4 cm) long, and vary in color from creamy white to dark brown. Although they are unsightly, they are actually quite harmless.

The life cycle of the cod worm is fascinating and complex. Adult cod worms live and mate inside the stomachs of gray seals, specifically gray seals that have eaten worm-infested fish. The cod worm's eggs pass out of the seal and into the ocean via the seal's feces. The eggs then hatch into tiny worm larvae that get eaten by small crustaceans such as shrimp. In turn, these small crustaceans get eaten by larger sea creatures, including fish such as cod and haddock. As the cod worm larvae reach the fish's stomach, they continue to grow, and eventually they burrow through the stomach wall and into the flesh of the fish. Finally, the cod worm's life cycle comes full circle when the fish is swallowed by another seal, and the process begins again.

it must be unpleasant to find a worm in your dinner

Although it must be quite unpleasant to find a worm in your dinner, cod worms are relatively harmless. The worms are killed by cooking or freezing the fish, and there is no evidence that anyone has ever had an illness associated with the cod worm. Occasionally, when you buy fresh fish, you might even find a live cod worm inside it. Although they're pretty gross, they are not toxic if eaten.

What Are Sweetbreads?

"Sweetbread" is a culinary term that refers to an animal's internal organs. The most commonly served sweetbreads are the thymus gland and pancreas, but chefs are also known to prepare the salivary and lymphatic glands. The thymus gland, which is known as the throat sweetbread, is found near the base of an animal's neck. The pancreas, which we call the heart sweetbread, is attached to the last rib and lies near the heart. Generally, the throat sweetbread of younger animals is preferred because of its firm texture and delicate flavor. Sweetbreads can be made from lamb, calf, and pig.

So why are they called sweetbreads? No one knows for sure, but thymus and pancreas would not be particularly appetizing-sounding words on a menu.

Do Flies Really Puke on Your Food **?**

The *Musca domestica*, better known as the common housefly, is found in almost every part of the world. It will eat almost anything, including rotting vegetables, animal carcasses, excrement, and vomit. This hairy, six-legged insect's mouthparts include a long proboscis, which is specially adapted for sucking up fluid or semifluid foods.

The fly has no problem eating thin fluids, such as milk or beer, or runny solids, such as poop, spit, or mucus. However, when the housefly's dinner consists of something rather more solid, such as dried blood, cheese, or cooked meats, it has to moisten the food first. It uses either spit or the

flies can carry more than a hundred types of disease-causing bacteria

regurgitated contents of a previous meal—perhaps some partially digested rotten trash or dog poop, for instance. This fly vomit contains an acid that helps to dissolve whatever the fly has landed on, making it possible for the fly to hoover it up.

There is another reason to keep flies off your food. The housefly has three pairs of legs, which end in claws and pad-like structures called the pulvilli. The pulvilli contain tiny, sticky hairs, which enable the fly to stick to even very smooth surfaces, such as glass. The pulvilli are also responsible for picking up harmful germs when the fly lands on things like dog poop, mucus, and rubbish. As a result, flies can carry more than a hundred types of disease-causing bacteria, including those that cause diarrhea, cholera, typhoid, and food poisoning.

What Is Maggot Cheese

Many of us enjoy cheeses that are riddled with mold, such as Stilton, but we would probably draw the line at a cheese infested with squirming mag-gots. But not the residents of Sardinia . . .

Casu marzu, which literally means "rotten cheese," is a Sardinian tradition that more than lives up to its name. It is traditionally made by putting sheep's milk cheese outside so flies can lay thousands of eggs into it. When these eggs hatch, they produce translucent white worms, which grow up to around a third of an inch (8 mm) long. These worms produce a substance that causes the fat in the cheese to putrefy. The brown, decomposing cheese becomes a soft, sticky mass that creates a spicy, burning sensation in the mouth when eaten.

Eating insect-ridden food can also present a different challenge—maggot larvae can leap dis-tances of up to 6 inches (15 cm) and have been known to jump into the cheese eater's eyes.

Because of the obvious health risks, casu marzu is officially outlawed in Italy, but it can still be bought on the black market. One official from the

Sardinian health department stated that anyone caught selling the cheese would be heavily fined, but admitted, "As a Sardinian and a man, let me tell you, I have never heard of anyone falling ill after eating this stuff. Sometimes, it tastes real good."

2
Disgusting Duties

What Is the Worst Job in History?

The annals of history are full of disgusting, dangerous, and demeaning jobs, but one of the most unpleasant has to have been that of the fuller. In the Middle Ages, this crummy job managed to combine grossness with mind-numbing boredom.

Fullers worked in the preparation of wool. After the sheep were sheared and the wool woven into cloth, a natural grease would remain in the wool. This grease made the cloth coarse and prevented a tight weave, so the job of the fuller was to get rid of the grease and other unwanted substances from the newly woven woolen cloth. To achieve this, the cloth was soaked in some kind of alkaline solution, and the cheapest alkaline solution available was stale urine, which is full of ammonia.

Of course, urine was always plentiful, and bucketfuls would be obtained from local houses, farms, and even public toilets. The next step was the tedious task of stamping on the cloth, while knee-deep in stale urine, for between seven and eight hours. The fuller would then rinse the cloth in clean water, take it outside, and stretch it out to dry.

> good thing
> **urine**
> was
> always
> **plentiful**

How Would a Tanner Use Dog Poop ?

Another unpleasant profession was that of the tanner during the Victorian era. Tanners were extremely skilled and respected, but the job was so smelly that tanners were required by law to set up their operations on the outskirts of town.

The tanning process would begin after a cow had been slaughtered and skinned. The tanner would clean the hide by soaking it in lime, then remove all the rotting meat and fat from it. (The fat was useful, since it could later be made into soap.) The cow's hair would also be removed by scraping it off with a knife. Next, to soften the leather, it would be soaked in a gross mixture called bate, which consisted of warmed-up water and feces, usually dogs' poop. Later, the hide was soaked in tanning fluid for a year, cleaned off, and finally dried out so that leather items could be made from it.

How Did a Tanner Get the Dog Poop ?

If the tanner's job sounds bad, spare a thought for his suppliers. Tanners needed a constant supply of dog poop, which was provided by somewhat lowlier workers called pure collectors. Their job was at least a simple one—they would roam the streets looking for dog poop, which they would scoop up, often with their bare hands, and then sell to tanners.

dog poop helped soften leather

What Was the Worst Part of Being a Squire ?

During the Middle Ages, a squire's job involved looking after his knight's every need, including caring for the knight's armor and weapons, helping him train, and helping him dress. But the worst part of the job was undoubtedly cleaning the knight's armor after a heavy day on the battlefield.

It took almost an hour to dress a knight in plate armor, which meant there were no quick toilet breaks while fighting. This meant that the knight not only sweated heavily, as tournaments mostly took place during the summer months, but also peed and pooped inside the armor.

Facing that part of the job was no fun, and to make matters worse, water was in short supply and far too precious to be used for trivial matters like cleaning. So the squire would instead have to

knights peed and pooped inside their armor

carry out this distasteful chore using an abrasive mixture of sand, vinegar, and urine.

What Were Gong Scourers ?

In the Tudor era (from the late 1400s to the early 1600s), there were no flushing toilets. Instead, King Henry VIII rested the royal posterior on what was called a close stool, which consisted of a bucket and water tank with a padded seat lavishly covered in black velvet. His groom of the stool was even required to wipe the royal bottom.

However, Henry's courtiers used communal facilities called the Great House of Easement at Hampton Court Palace, a two-story lavatory with rows of oak planks with holes cut in the wood at two-foot intervals. Chutes made of bricks or stone would carry the waste down to a basin, which then flowed directly into the River Thames. However, some of the more solid waste would collect in the brick chambers, which had to be regularly cleaned.

This stinky task was given to gong scourers, who were also known as gongfermors or gong farmers.

gong scourers were often young boys

The gong scourers were often young boys, since they were small enough to crawl along the drains.

What Job Included Tasting Dirt?

In the sixteenth century in England, it was the trade of the saltpeter man to extract potassium nitrates, also known as saltpeter, from feces and urine. Saltpeter was an important ingredient in gunpowder, so to ensure that the supply stayed high, the saltpeter men were given a license from the king to go into anyone's home and dig wherever they saw fit. They would search houses, barns, stables, outhouses, cellars, latrines, pigpens, and manure heaps, collect any poop, and dig out the sewage-ridden earth of the cesspit. They would cart it all away in barrels.

How, you may wonder, would they know where to dig? Well, often their sense of smell would tell them, but where there was doubt, the saltpeter men would identify which parts of the soil were rich in saltpeter by tasting it.

What Was the Unpleasant Job of a Decrotteur ?

The word *decrotteur* means "scraper," and the job meant just about the worst kind of scraping you could think of.

In the 1700s, Paris was the world's cultural hub: the center of science, art, fashion, and generally a city of exquisite taste. But according to Jean-Jacques Rousseau, the eighteenth-century French philosopher, in the courthouse, in the museum, at the opera, even at the palace of Versailles, "one does not know where to sit in summer, without inhaling the odor of stagnant urine." Courtyards, corridors, and alleys would be full of urine and feces. In addition, chamber pots containing human waste were often emptied out of windows. The person emptying the pot would call out, "*Garde l'eau!*" which means, "Look out for the water!" though everyone knew it wasn't just water flying down. Pedestrians also had to watch out for speeding carriages to avoid being splashed with trash and raw sewage.

chamber pots containing **human waste** were often **emptied** out of **windows**

What was a person to do if attending some sophisticated event at which an outfit matted with excrement might be frowned upon? Luckily, Parisian high society had a solution for this problem. The grand houses would employ a decrotteur to clean the muck off of the shoes and stockings of new arrivals before they entered.

What Was a Dredgerman?

In the late 1800s, the River Thames in London was covered with slime and full of sewage. As disgusting as

the River Thames in London was full of sewage

the river was, the Thames provided many poor Londoners with a living. The dredgerman's job involved fishing for corpses.

In those days, dredgermen were kept busy. They were paid for each corpse they found, and often made more money by taking anything valuable from the dead before handing the body over to the authorities.

Another similarly unpleasant job of the time was that of the mud lark, although calling it a job may be something of a stretch. Mud larks were scavengers who spent their time trawling the banks of the Thames, looking for anything of value. In those days, it was common to see old women foraging along the riverbank, carrying a basket or a tin kettle, into which they would put anything of value they might find. It was not just a job for women either—small children as young as seven years old would also be found searching through the filth. They poked around in the wet mud for small pieces of coal, chips of wood, bits of old rope, bones, or more valuable debris such as copper nails.

Mud larks often had to wade up to their midriffs through excrement and mud while scavenging on the banks of the River Thames. They were too poor to buy decent clothing, so they wore filthy rags and didn't wear shoes. Consequently, it was common for them to injure themselves, or catch infections, by stepping on nails or glass. If a mud lark didn't find anything she could sell before the tide rose, she would most likely go hungry until the next tide went out.

3
Vile Bodies

What Underwear Blocks the Smell of Farts ?

Let's face it, everyone farts, and studies have shown that when men and women eat the same food, women produce more concentrated gas than men—in other words, stinkier farts!

One inventive husband decided he wanted to take action. Buck Weimer of Pueblo, Colorado, set to work to find a way to prevent the odor of his wife's farts from taking over the bedroom.

Buck had the idea of using a filter to absorb any bad smells. He experimented with the filters used in the gas masks worn by coal miners—he put one into his pants, and although it didn't work perfectly, he knew he was on the right track. He worked on different versions for six years and then came up with a brand-new invention: Under-Ease—airtight underwear with a replaceable charcoal filter that removes bad-smelling gases before they can escape (unfortunately, they don't prevent the noise). So no one could steal his revolutionary new idea, Buck received a patent in 1998.

Buck's Under-Ease underwear are made from a soft, nylon-type fabric with elastic around the waist and legs. The removable filter, which looks a bit like a shoulder pad, is made of charcoal sandwiched between two layers of Australian sheep's wool. Buck claims that the multilayered filter pad traps the 1–2% of human gas that creates the foul smell (mostly hydrogen sulfide), but allows the remaining non-smelling gas to pass through. It also allows the natural buildup of body heat to pass through. The underwear can be worn anytime, anywhere—at night, at parties, on airplanes. And thankfully, they are machine washable.

> **Under-Ease can't contain the sound of farts**

The company's motto is "Wear them for the ones you love."

Who Was the Fart Maniac?

In the 1800s, a French baker named Joseph Pujol (1857–1945) had a second job in the theater. He took to the stage, often wearing clothing that exposed his bottom, and made a lot of money entertaining large audiences with various tunes, all produced by farting.

His stage name was Le Pétomane, which literally means "the fart maniac," and his remarkable talents included imitating various sounds and doing party tricks with his farts. Using a rubber tube, he was able to blow out a candle 12 inches (30.5 cm) away just by bending over and farting. Also, he could even play a couple of tunes on a flute.

In 1892, he entertained audiences at Paris's Moulin Rouge. He would begin with a series of quiet farts, saying they came from a little girl, then a mother-in-law, and then a bride on her wedding

he could even play a couple of tunes on a flute

night. He'd build up to very loud ones that could go for about ten seconds. He completed the performance by mimicking the sound of cannon fire, producing an impressively loud, booming noise.

What Were Waterloo Teeth ?

At the Battle of Waterloo in 1815, so many lives were lost that there were rich pickings for the British troops when the battle was over. The dead were stripped of anything of value—including their teeth. Such a vast number of teeth were extracted from the dead at Waterloo that for many years afterward, dentures were known as Waterloo teeth. A tooth transplant involved taking a tooth from one person and transplanting it into the head of another person, and many people unwittingly wore teeth extracted from the soldiers.

Tooth transplants plummeted in popularity when it was discovered that infections could be transmitted in this way.

Which Disease Caused Its Victims' Organs to Liquefy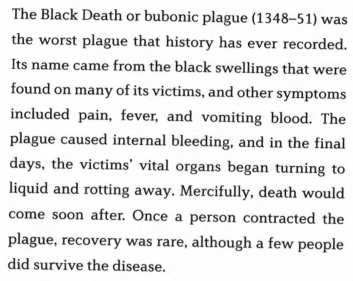

The Black Death or bubonic plague (1348–51) was the worst plague that history has ever recorded. Its name came from the black swellings that were found on many of its victims, and other symptoms included pain, fever, and vomiting blood. The plague caused internal bleeding, and in the final days, the victims' vital organs began turning to liquid and rotting away. Mercifully, death would come soon after. Once a person contracted the plague, recovery was rare, although a few people did survive the disease.

The Black Death was responsible for killing up to half the people in Europe, and struck England in 1348. It was at its worst in cities, where there was enormous overcrowding and poor hygiene and sanitation. When the plague reached London, tens of thousands of people died—nearly half of the city's population. Over the period of the

Black Death, the population of England went from around 6 million to 3 million. So many perished that the graveyards were soon full and corpses had to be buried in fields.

Plague epidemics occurred regularly across Europe following the Black Death. The last outbreak of plague in England was the Great Plague of 1665. As in 1348, the plague spread quickly and killed many people. The plague's victims developed painful pus-filled swellings, or buboes, which usually meant the person would die.

To help ensure victims did not pass on the infection, the British government forced them to stay in their houses, and their doors were nailed shut and marked with a large red cross. Searchers were paid to remove corpses of victims from homes, and walked around streets calling, "Bring out your dead!" As more people became sick, the rich left the city and most of the doctors and clergy went with them. The poor, on the other hand, were not allowed to leave, as they were seen as the carriers of the disease and could infect others.

The Great Plague claimed around 100,000 victims.

Experts believe that the Great Plague was caused by a bacterium called *Yersinia pestis*, which lived inside fleas. These fleas were carried by black rats, and when the flea bit a person, it would transfer the bacteria, and therefore the plague, to the victim. However, some experts take a different view. They argue that because the Black Death spread so quickly, it must have been caused by a virus that could be passed from person to person, like the disease Ebola, which also causes massive internal bleeding.

What Is the Worst Sound in the World?

It's official—the most unpleasant sound in the world is that of a person vomiting. A survey was carried out to identify the world's worst sound, and, perhaps unsurprisingly, vomiting was voted as the sound that made most people want to cover their ears. The sound was re-created by an actor using a diluted bucket of baked beans to mimic the sound of vomit cascading into a toilet.

> the sound was re-created using a bucket of baked beans

The study, set up by Trevor Cox, a professor of acoustic engineering at Salford University in Manchester, England, asked for people's opinions on thirty-four sounds. The survey attracted more than 1.1 million votes from around the world. People listened to sounds, such as a dentist's drill, fingernails scraping down a blackboard, and an aircraft flying past, before rating them in order of offensiveness. Microphone feedback was judged to be the second most unpleasant sound, followed by the sounds of babies crying and the scrapes and squeaks of a train on a track.

What Causes the Stench of B.O.?

Body odor is the unpleasant smell produced by a person's body if they don't wash often enough. Adults have more than 2 million sweat glands with pores on the skin's surface. Sweat comes out of the pores and onto the skin, where it evaporates to help keep the body cool. Interestingly, sweat itself has no odor at all. But when sweat comes into contact with the bacteria on your skin, you can wind up with a terrible smell. There is also a special type of sweat gland, called an apocrine gland, found only under the arms and between the legs. These glands produce a thicker liquid than the body's other sweat glands, and the warm conditions in those areas can lead to stronger body odor.

Infrequent washing of the skin and hair can cause dirt, dead skin cells, and dried sweat to collect—particularly under the arms. This provides food for bacteria, which then release a foul odor. Fungi can also grow on dirty skin, and these can cause illness. For example, a condition called athlete's foot is caused by a fungus that attacks the skin between the toes, and in more severe cases it can spread over the whole foot. It causes the skin to peel off the foot, leaving itchy, sore patches. Fungi can also affect the nails, resulting in an unsightly discoloration, crumbling, and separation of the nail. As well as the risks from bacteria and fungi, dirty skin also makes an ideal breeding ground for lice, mites, and fleas. So the message is clear—scrub up!

dirt, dead skin cells, and dried sweat are food for bacteria

How Many Insect Parts Do We Unintentionally Eat?

Few of the people who read this book will ever deliberately sit down to a meal of fried hairy caterpillars or chocolate-covered cockroaches. However, even if we may not actively choose to eat insects, insect parts will crop up in our food whether we like it or not. According to estimates, the average person consumes about two pounds (1 kg) of insects every year.

Virtually everything we eat has bugs (entire or parts) within. When crops are harvested, farmers can't help but collect some insects as well. There are actually government standards for the maximum number of bug parts per unit for each type of food.

virtually everything we eat has bugs within

The U.S. Food and Drug Administration's (FDA) "Food Action Defect Levels" hand-book itemizes the "levels of natural or unavoidable defects in foods that present no health hazards for humans." The following is a list of foods and the amount of insect parts, rodent parts, and other general unpleasantness that is allowed to be contained within them.

- Chocolate may contain up to sixty insect fragments per 100 grams, and an average of less than one rodent hair per 100 grams.

- Pasta products are allowed up to 225 insect fragments per 225 grams, and no more than four and a half rodent hairs per 225 grams.

- Peanut butter should contain fewer than thirty insect fragments per 100 grams, and an average of less than one rodent hair per 100 grams.

- Canned tomatoes may contain up to ten fly eggs per 500 grams, and no more than two maggots per 500 grams.

- Wheat should average less than 9 milligrams of rodent excreta pellets, and/or pellet fragments, per kilogram.

Which Room Contains the Most Germs— the Bathroom or the Kitchen?

Dr. Charles Gerba, known as "Dr. Germ" by his colleagues, is a microbiologist at the University of

Arizona. Dr. Germ is renowned for being America's expert on domestic and public hygiene, and has appeared on numerous television programs. He has made quite a name for himself studying public toilets and other places where germs hang out.

Dr. Germ carried out a survey and found that in most homes, the bathroom is usually cleaner than the kitchen. Surprisingly, the least contaminated place in either room was the toilet seat. Accordingly, Dr. Germ concluded that most people would be safer making a sandwich on a toilet seat than on the kitchen counter.

Moist environments in the kitchen, such as the sink drain, were some of the most contaminated with bacteria. However, the worst offender is the kitchen sponge or dishcloth, which can contain up to 50 million bacteria! Dr. Germ found that kitchen sinks are the place where you can find the worst kinds of germs,

Surprise! the bathroom is usually cleaner than the kitchen

and thorough wiping of sink and counters with a sponge or dishcloth serves only to spread them all over the kitchen.

Ironically, it may be that the people who try hardest to keep their kitchen clean are those in the most danger. Dr. Germ explains, "Clean people are usually the dirtiest, because they spread the germs all around. The bachelor who never cleans is usually the cleanest from a germ standpoint." If you want to actually clean your kitchen, rather than simply pushing the germs around, Dr. Germ recommends using an antibacterial spray and paper towels. However, most people who use their kitchens every day rarely get infected with anything, because most of the germs are fairly harmless and the body's immune system helps to fight off any that cause trouble.

How Clean Is Your Toothbrush

It would seem reasonable to assume that your toothbrush is fairly clean, wouldn't it? After all, it gets rinsed twice a day, and toothpaste kills germs, right? However, chances are that your toothbrush is full of bacteria and fungi.

It may surprise you, but bacteria can thrive on toothbrushes, since the tools provide germs with lots of food and water. Researchers have found many different types of bacteria as well as viruses on used toothbrushes. It is also not a good idea to use somebody else's used toothbrush—research has shown that infections can spread that way. A brand-new toothbrush becomes contaminated the first time you use it, and bacteria and viruses from one brush can easily spread to another. However, it isn't actually clear how much of a danger this poses in the everyday life of a healthy person. And the good news is that most toothbrush germs disappear when the toothbrush has thoroughly dried out.

> chances are your toothbrush is full of bacteria and fungi

It also makes a big difference where you keep your toothbrush. A study in the journal *Applied Microbiology* showed that there is a risk of contamination if your toothbrush is positioned near the toilet. When we flush, water droplets spray into the air. It has been found that these water droplets can travel as far as 20 feet (6 m) from the toilet. One solution is to put the lid down before flushing the toilet, but this will only mean the bacteria will instead be found on the underside of the toilet lid. Still, probably better that than having them on your toothbrush!

Who Has the World's Longest Ear Hair?

According to *The Guinness Book of World Records,* the person with the world's longest ear hair is Anthony Victor, who lives in India. At its longest point, Mr. Victor's ear hair measures over 7 inches (18 cm). Other revolting and unusual records include the following:

- The longest leg hair belongs to Wesley Pemberton, who lives in the United States; it measures 6.5 inches (16.5 cm) long.

- The record for the world's loudest burp belongs to Paul Hunn, who lives in the United Kingdom. Hunn set his record in 2009 by letting out an ear-splitting burp of 109.9 decibels, equivalent to a jet engine at take-off.

- Kim Goodman of the United States can pop her eyeballs almost a half an inch (12 mm) beyond her eye sockets. This astonishing feat was measured in Istanbul, Turkey, in 2007.

- In 2001, Ken Edwards, who lives in the UK, set a record in London by eating thirty-six cockroaches in one minute.

> **Ken Edwards ate thirty-six cockroaches in one minute**

- The world's longest tongue belongs to Stephen Taylor of the United Kingdom. It measures 3.86 inches (9.8 cm) from its tip to the center of his closed top lip.

- Until recently, the longest fingernails in the world belonged to a lady named Lee Redmond of the United States, who had not cut her nails since 1979. She had a total nail length of 28 feet 4.5 inches (8.65 m). Her longest nail, on her right thumb, was 2 feet 11 inches (90 cm) long. However, in February 2009, Redmond was involved in a car crash and her nails were damaged beyond repair.

4

They Did What?!

What Did Hippocrates Think Pigeon Droppings Could Do?

Hippocrates was an ancient Greek physician who is widely regarded as the "father of medicine" and the founder of a more modern, scientific approach to illness that rejected superstition and divine influence. One of Hippocrates's more unusual recommendations was that bald men should apply pigeon droppings to their bald spots, to encourage the hair to regrow. This may sound bizarre, but it is just one of many crazy cures for baldness that have been suggested throughout history.

The ancient Egyptians, for example, recommended the application of rotten crocodile or hippo fat, thinking that the bad smell would stimulate growth.

Ancient Romans had an ingenious use for houseflies. They thought that if they mashed them up into a paste, which was then applied onto a bald spot, the hair would grow back. Julius Caesar was said to have been follicularly challenged, so Cleopatra applied a substance containing ground horse teeth and deer marrow to his bald spots.

And the wacky remedies didn't die out with the ancient world. Even as recently as the late 1800s, desperate men were applying chicken feces to their bald spots and encouraging cows to lick their heads!

What Caused Members of Parliament to Flee the Houses of Parliament in 1858 ?

In the 1850s, London was a pretty disgusting place. It was greatly overpopulated, and the sanitation was poor. The streets, streams, and rivers were choked with sewage, and much of the waste from sinks and toilets ran down old sewers straight into the River Thames. Since most Londoners also got their drinking water from the Thames, it's hardly surprising that many people became sick and even died as a result.

During the long, hot summer of 1858, the people of central London were plagued by a foul stench. The summer was so dry that much of the water in the Thames evaporated, and river levels became very low. This meant that sewage dumped into the river was not carried out to sea, so it became an open sewer. Also, for years, slaughterhouse waste, trash, dead animals, chemicals from factories, and even dead bodies had been dumped in the Thames. As this horrid stew baked in the sun, the stench became unbearable, and the disgusting odor could be smelled from sixty miles away.

> the disgusting **odor** could be **smelled from sixty** miles away

Sanitation workers deposited tons of lime into the river to help combat the foul stench, and lime-soaked curtains were hung in the windows of Parliament, which sits on the bank of the river. Eventually the stink got so bad that members of Parliament fled from the building. Heavy rain finally broke the hot weather and restored the river to normal levels.

What Is the Medicinal Use of Hangman's Rope?

Before the development of modern medicine, many illnesses were treated in ways that we now consider superstitious, wrongheaded, or just plain bizarre. For example, in the 1700s, it was believed that the way to cure a headache was to tie a piece of hangman's rope around your skull. Luckily for the hangmen, this was a period in which there were regular public hangings, giving them an easy second income. The following are a number of other strange remedies from the past:

cow dung

- Cow dung was a traditional cure for skin conditions, such as ulcers, inflammation, abscesses, and boils.

urine

- The book *Old-Fashioned Remedies* recommends, "When your feet are sweaty and aching, or if you have got athlete's foot, blisters or bruises, soak your feet in a bowl of hot urine."

soak your **feet** in a bowl of **hot urine**

frog spit

- It was widely believed that a wart could be cured if it was rubbed with frog spit or snails, which should then be impaled on the thorns of bushes. Licking the eyes of a frog was recommended for eye complaints.

insects

- To help treat a fever, it was recommended to eat woodlice, sometimes called pill bugs. Consuming a spider was also believed to help bring down a fever, as was keeping a spider in a bag and hanging it around your neck.

plague

- There were numerous daft suggestions to help ward off the plague, including the following:

> - Keep dirty goats in your home.
>
> - Fart into a container, and release it when the plague is near.
>
> - Smoke tobacco—children as young as three were ordered to smoke, for their own safety.
>
> - Press a dead, dried toad against swollen lymph glands.

Did Little Miss Muffet Really Eat Mashed-Up Spiders?

> *Little Miss Muffet*
> *Sat on a tuffet,*
> *Eating her curds and whey;*
> *Along came a spider,*
> *Who sat down beside her*
> *And frightened Miss Muffet away.*

The origin of this nursery rhyme is uncertain. "Little Miss Muffet" first appeared in print in Scotland in 1805, although it was probably around for a lot longer. Some historians believe that the nursery rhyme is based on a little girl called Patience, whose stepfather was an eminent English doctor called Thomas Muffet (1553–1604).

Thomas Muffet was passionate about bugs, especially spiders, and how they related to medicine. He was a strong believer in the power of spiders to cure nearly any ailment. Most of his remedies consisted of eating spiders, but some were more imaginative. For example, Dr. Muffet's recommended treatment for cuts or abrasions was to wrap the wound in fresh spiderwebs, which apparently worked quite well.

He is thought to have instructed Patience to eat mashed spiders to recover from colds (in fact, this was a fairly common remedy for colds two hundred years ago), leading to the fear of spiders highlighted in the nursery rhyme.

What Did a Goat's Tongue Have to Do With Medieval Prisoners ?

tickling torture was not funny

In the Middle Ages, there were a range of clever and inventive torture methods designed to punish or force a confession out of you. In a punishment known as the goat's tongue, or tickling torture, the victim's feet would be placed into wooden stocks and covered with salt or a sweet substance.

Goats love salt, and for hours will happily continue to lick feet that are covered in it. Although the sensation starts out as initially being little more than a tickle, pain soon follows, as the goat's rough tongue causes the soles of the feet to blister and become sore. Sometimes the goat's tongue would reach bone before a prisoner would confess. Vlad the Impaler of Transylvania enjoyed using this torture on Turkish prisoners. Salt water would be continually dripped onto their feet from above, and enthusiastic goats would be released.

Another unpleasant torture technique of the Middle Ages was the rack. This nifty device was used to extract confessions, and was introduced to the Tower of London in about 1420 by the Duke of Exeter. The torture rack consisted of a strong wooden frame fitted with a large roller at each end. The prisoner would lay on the frame with ropes attaching the rollers to his ankles and wrists. If the prisoner did not confess to his crime, the rollers would be turned, pulling the limbs in opposite directions. The body would be stretched until the joints of the limbs would eventually become dislocated, resulting in excruciating pain. This method was also used with great relish during the Spanish Inquisition.

Guy Fawkes (1570–1606) was put on the rack in 1605. He was tortured for ten days at the Tower of London until he gave up the names of the other members of the Gunpowder Plot. He was so severely injured that he had to be carried to the scaffold for his execution.

During the reign of Elizabeth I, many Catholic priests were executed as traitors. English Jesuit Edmund Campion (1540–81) was jailed for heresy, after refusing to give up his Catholicism. He was tortured, but even when iron spikes were driven under his fingernails and toenails, he refused to give in. He was later placed on the rack, which caused extreme agony, but he still refused to confess. It is said that when he came off the rack, he was 4 inches (10 cm) taller than before. Campion was given a final chance to renounce his Catholic faith in exchange for his freedom, but his loyalty to the Pope proved too strong. In 1581, Campion was executed as a traitor and hanged, drawn, and quartered at Tyburn, London.

Thumbscrews were handy, pocket-sized contraptions that were highly effective at inflicting excruciating pain. The victim's fingers were placed inside the instrument and slowly crushed as the torturer turned the handle on top. Some cunning thumbscrews even had little studs inserted inside them, to increase the suffering of the victim. An overenthusiastic torturer would sometimes crush the finger to a pulpy mess! In Scotland, thumbscrews were known by the rather cute name of thumbkins, and were used until the end of the seventeenth century.

The same instrument was also used to crush victims' toes, and even bigger variants were used to crush victims' feet, knees, and elbows. Another devious device was the head crusher, which, as you might imagine, was designed for applying pressure to the head.

Why Did the Chinese Bind the Feet of Young Girls ?

Until fairly recently, the Chinese had a long tradition of binding the feet of young girls. Small feet were highly prized as a mark of great beauty. Since women tend to have smaller feet than men, it was felt that the smaller a woman's feet, the more feminine she was.

Foot binding went on for almost a thousand years and only began to die out at the beginning of the twentieth century. Foot binding was prohibited in China in 1911, but continued in isolated regions well into the 1930s. Young girls would have their feet bound from the age of about seven. The girl's mother and other close female relatives would tightly wrap each foot in bandages, sparing only the big toe, which pointed upward. The other toes would be bent into the sole of the foot and the sole and the heel would be bound as close together as possible. The bindee would then be made to walk so that the bones in her toes and arches would break and keep the new shape. Every few weeks, the bound feet would be squeezed into smaller and smaller shoes. This was an excruciatingly painful process, and the girls would suffer pain for about a year. Eventually, however, their feet simply became numb. The goal was for the girl to have a foot that measured as little as 3.5 inches (9 cm) long.

Naturally, the girls' feet would become grossly deformed, which meant they would hobble when they walked, if they could walk at all—many had to be carried.

After the Execution of King Charles I, Why Did People Dab Their Hankies into His Blood?

Charles I (1600–49) was a deeply unpopular English king who inspired two civil wars. After the second, he was captured, tried, and found guilty of making war on his own people. He was sentenced to be executed in 1649.

As the ax came down upon his neck, there was a groan from the crowd. The axman then held Charles's head up to the crowd, and blood splattered everywhere. After paying a fee, people hurriedly dipped their handkerchiefs in the king's blood and took hairs from his head and beard. They also scraped up bloody earth from beneath the scaffold.

> people took
> **hairs**
> from his head
> **and beard**

People believed that royalty had godlike powers and thought that the king's blood would cure their wounds and illnesses. They wiped their blood-soaked hankies onto wounds, and some people dabbed them over themselves, one another, and their sick children.

Whose Head Was Shown Off for Nearly Thirty Years after His Death?

Celebrated English adventurer Sir Walter Raleigh (1554–1618) was a key figure in popularizing tobacco smoking in Britain. During the 1500s, tobacco was seldom used for pleasure but was seen as a cure-all to treat almost every illness imaginable—everything from skin complaints to gangrenous limbs. Raleigh specifically promoted and sold tobacco to the rich. The upper classes embraced the habit of pipe smoking, and Raleigh made a lot of money.

King James VI of Scotland not only disliked smoking but also hated Raleigh. When he became King of England in 1603, he had Raleigh, who was a Protestant, arrested and tried as a conspirator in a planned Catholic uprising. Raleigh was found guilty and sentenced to death, even though the evidence was flimsy.

Raleigh was beheaded in 1618 at the age of sixty-four, and his body was buried in St. Margaret's Church, next to Westminster Abbey. However, his head was put into a red leather bag and given to his widow, Elizabeth. She had Raleigh's head embalmed and is said to have carried it around with her wherever she went. Apparently, when people came to visit her at home, she would ask them if they'd like to see Walter. If they agreed, she would bring it out of the bag. She con-

his **head** was put into a red leather bag

tinued carrying the head around right up to her death twenty-nine years later. But that was not the end of the story, because, even after Elizabeth's death, her son Carew continued the tradition, carrying his father's head with him everywhere he went. When Carew eventually died in 1666, Sir Walter Raleigh's head was buried with him, in West Horsley, Surrey.

5
Weird Creatures

Why Does the Horned Lizard Squirt Blood from Its Eyes ?

Thirteen species of horned lizard are found in North America, and they have broad bodies and rough skin, with horns on their head and spines across their back. Although they look quite frightening, horned lizards are usually docile and passive unless provoked, and they have a rather gross way of fending off predators.

Despite their spiky, unappetizing features, horned lizards are preyed upon by a wide range of creatures, including hawks, roadrunners, snakes, dogs, wolves, coyotes, and other lizards. To defend themselves against these numerous threats, the horned lizard has developed a number of remarkable and unusual talents. When faced with a hungry predator, the horned lizard is able to inflate itself with air so that it resembles a spiky balloon, making it look bigger and more threatening.

If this doesn't work, the lizard can employ another bizarre technique—shooting blood from its eyes. It arches its back defensively and closes its eyes. The blood pressure inside the lizard's head quickly rises, and this pressure causes blood vessels in the sinuses to rupture. Then the lizard's eyeballs become infused with blood and swell up, causing the eyelids to bulge. Finally, the swollen eyelids, engorged with blood, send out a fine spray of blood through the tear ducts. They can shoot blood from either one or both eyes, up to a distance of 6 feet (2 m), and they can even direct the spray forward or backward.

a fine spray of blood flies from the tear ducts

So what's the point of this extraordinary ability? Well, first, the blood squirting serves to alarm and confuse would-be predators, naturally enough. Another benefit is that the stream of blood contains a chemical that dogs, wolves, and coyotes find disgusting. If any of these dogs gets the blood in its mouth, it gets distracted because the substance so repulsive.

However, despite having these spectacular

talents, the horned lizards' most effective way of avoiding predators is simply to lie still. The lizards' coloring is similar to that of their environment, and they can get rid of any shadows by flattening their bodies against the ground. If they have to move, they can run and then stop suddenly and unexpectedly, lying flat to merge into their surroundings, leaving the predator scratching its head, wondering where its dinner went.

Which Worm May Crawl out of Your Nose?

Worldwide, about 1.4 billion people have one or more *Ascaris* worms living inside them. However, they rarely cause a problem, so people don't realize they're playing host to an uninvited guest.

The most commonly encountered parasitic worm is the *Ascaris lumbricoides*, called a roundworm, which can measure up to 14 inches (35.5 cm) in length. So how do they find their way into our bodies? The eggs of *Ascaris* are transmitted in feces and find their way into a new host via food or dirty fingers.

Once inside the body, the eggs hatch into larvae within a person's stomach, before moving into the small intestine. They then penetrate through the intestinal wall, enter the blood circulation, and are carried around the body. The larvae make their way to the lungs, and as they continue to climb, the young *Ascaris* larvae tend to slightly irritate the airways as they crawl up the back of the throat, which can cause a cough reflex, resulting in a free ride into the throat. Occasionally adult worms can be coughed up into the mouth too, which gives the sufferer quite a shock. From the throat, the larvae are swallowed, which brings them to the intestines, where they make their home and grow into adult worms.

> adult **worms** can be **coughed up** into the mouth

Adult worms can live in a person's gut for about six to twenty-four months, and many people are unaware of their infestation until they see an adult worm in their poop or cough one up. The worms have even also been known to come out of a person's nose or in their vomit. In severe cases, where people host many worms, the victim may suffer from anemia or even malnutrition. The *Ascaris* worm is estimated to affect 4 million people in the United States.

Which Fish Uses Slime to Kill Its Enemies?

When a creature has not one disgusting name but two, the odds are against it being a cute, doe-eyed bundle of fur. Such is the case with the hagfish, also known as the slime eel, which is every bit as disgusting as these names suggest. The hagfish is an ancient creature that has been around for 300 million years. It is virtually blind and resembles an oversized, slimy worm. Hagfish are

the hagfish has been around for 300 million years

completely covered in mucus, which oozes out of hundreds of slime pores found on the sides of their bodies.

The hagfish hangs around on the bottom of the ocean floor and looks for fish that are either sick or dead. It then climbs inside its prey through the mouth, gill, eye socket, or anus, and devours it from the inside out, using its tooth-covered tongue to scrape its victim to pieces.

When faced with a predator, the hagfish uses its glands to produce slime that quickly turns the surrounding water thick and gunky. Described as rubbery snot, this slime surrounds the predator and can even kill it by clogging up its gills and suffocating it. However, there is a delicate balance to be struck, as the hagfish must be careful not to produce so much mucus that it suffocates itself. When the hagfish thinks that the coast is clear, it will tie itself into knots to rub away the excess slime.

Fishermen consider hagfish a nuisance because they penetrate the bodies of fish caught in the fishermen's nets and eat them from the inside out, leaving nothing but skin and bones. One large fish was found with more than one hundred hagfish munching inside it.

What Is
the Hagfish's Even Uglier Cousin

A close relative of the hagfish is the lamprey. The lamprey has a slimy, eel-like body and can grow up to 4 feet (1.2 m) in length. It has two fins along its back, a single nostril in the middle of the head, and a most unpleasant mouth. The lamprey's large, funnel-like mouth is very round, with rows of razor-sharp teeth, a sharp tongue, and lips that also bear many rasping teeth. Unlike the hagfish, the lamprey chooses healthy creatures to feed on, including human beings.

When a lamprey comes across a potential victim, which could be another fish or a swimmer with cold legs, it attacks by attaching its sucking lips onto the skin of the victim. Its sharp teeth scrape open a wound, and then the toothed tongue goes into action, lapping the blood and body fluids of the victim. The lamprey has a special type of saliva that stops the prey's blood from clotting, so it can feast for a long time. Once the lamprey has eaten its fill, it lets go. The victim doesn't die from the bite itself, but it bears a wound that may become infected. Where lampreys are common, a single host fish may have several lampreys attached to it at one time. And if a fish suffers too many lamprey attacks, it may become weak and die. Infected lamprey bites cause the deaths of many fish in the ocean and the Great Lakes. However, human victims are fairly rare, with no recorded fatalities.

Which Animal Is the Best Actor

One of nature's most impressive and convincing performances is that given by the North American opossum (*Didelphis virginiana*), a small mammal found throughout the United States. Opossums usually live in woodlands and reach about 20 inches (51 cm) long. They are mostly gray-colored, with a white, pointed face and a tail like a rat's but bigger. They are active at night and will eat almost anything: insects, snails, toads, rodents, and even dead animals.

opossums will eat almost anything, even dead animals

The main threats faced by opossums are dogs, cats, foxes, and people. When they feel threatened, opossums will hiss and bear their many sharp teeth. If this doesn't work, they may use their considerable acting skills by playing dead. The opossum will flop down on its side, lying still, with its eyes half closed, its mouth hanging open, and its tongue lolling out of its mouth. If required, it can play dead for several hours; even if it is poked or kicked it will not move a muscle. For added verisimilitude, the opossum may even defecate on itself, as well as release a foul-smelling green slime that smells like rotting flesh. Most of the opossum's predators will not eat animals that are already dead, so they leave the stinking opossum alone.

Why Do Skunks Stink ?

The skunk is a member of the weasel family, which is commonly found in North America. Skunks rarely attack unless they are cornered or defending their young. But if a skunk does feel threatened and is unable to escape, it will put on an aggressive display by growling, fluffing up its fur, shaking its tail, stamping the ground with its front feet, standing on its hind legs, and spitting violently, all of which will hopefully serve to frighten and discourage the potential attacker. However, if those methods don't work and the predator remains a threat, the skunk will lift up its tail and spray.

The chemical skunks spray at their enemies is a sulfur compound called N-bulymercaptan, which burns the attacker's skin and causes stinging in the eyes, making the predator blind for a short while.

skunk spray burns the attacker's skin and causes stinging in the eyes

The skunk sprays this disgusting, noxious chemical in a fanlike pattern from two small openings near its rear end, which act rather like tiny water pistols. A skunk can aim this spray in all directions, but they seldom spray without being provoked or giving warning. The skunk's spray is extremely accurate and effective at a range of up to 15 feet (4.6 m). As a result, even though skunks have sharp teeth, they rarely use them in defense.

If it gets into a person's eyes, skunk spray is extremely irritating and can cause temporary blindness but no permanent damage.

Which Wasp Lays Its Eggs inside a Caterpillar?

There is a tiny wasp called *Cotesia congregata*, commonly found in the United States, that has a deeply unpleasant, although clever, way of helping her eggs to hatch, which also ensures the little ones have a ready-made meal waiting for them.

The victim of this unpleasant practice is the large green *Manduca sexta* caterpillar, which is more commonly known as the tobacco hornworm. Because of its green color, this caterpillar is often overlooked by predators when hidden in a plant's leaves. But this wasp hunts by smell, and the smell of the caterpillar's feces guides the wasp to its prey. It then lands on the back of the caterpillar, punctures its hide, and uses its tubelike stinger to inject as many as several hundred eggs into the victim's body. A few days later, wasp larvae emerge from the eggs and begin to grow. As the larvae near maturity, they chew their way through the body of the dying caterpillar and spin cocoons on its back.

> the smell of the caterpillar's feces guides the wasp to its prey

However, there is a danger that the caterpillar's potent defenses could kill the wasp's offspring, so the wasp has to disable them. Furthermore, the wasp must do this without killing the caterpillar, otherwise the wasp larvae will die too. Therefore, the wasp needs to keep the caterpillar alive but defenseless. To achieve this, when laying her eggs, the wasp injects the caterpillar with venom that includes a virus. This virus produces toxic proteins that disable the caterpillar's immune system and hamper its physical growth, making it easier for the wasp larvae to take over. Gross but clever!

Is It True That a Cockroach Farts Every Fifteen Minutes

There are more than 3,500 types of cockroaches of all shapes and sizes. The hissing cockroach from Madagascar is as big as a mouse, while the smallest cockroaches are the size of a tomato seed.

the hissing **cockroach** from **Madagascar is as big as a mouse**

Until recently, a beast called the giant burrowing cockroach held the record for the world's largest roach. This wingless cockroach, which bizarrely is a popular pet in Australia, grows up to 3.5 inches (9 cm) long—about the size of an adult finger—and weighs more than 1.5 ounces, which is about the weight of an AA battery. Despite its large size, it's able to flatten its body so it can fit into the smallest spaces. However, in 2004, scientists exploring caves in Borneo discovered a new species of cockroach. The monster roach measured 4 inches (10 cm) long, and this new discovery has taken over as the world's largest roach in terms of size, although the giant burrowing cockroach is still the world's heaviest.

Besides eating just about anything, including the toe jam on your feet, the moisture in your nostrils, the sweat in your armpits, and even their own skins or other cockroaches, another gross habit is farting. On average, they break wind every fifteen minutes. They also continue to release stinky methane gas for eighteen hours after they die. Insects called termites also fart a great deal and, along with cockroaches, are believed to be among the biggest contributors to global warming.

cockroaches are believed to be among the biggest contributors to global warming

Cockroaches are also some of nature's hardiest creatures. Some species of cockroach can survive in blazing heat, while others can endure being frozen, then thawed, and still crawl away unharmed. Some cockroaches can go without food for three weeks. This astonishing creature can even survive for up to nine days after being decapitated. It can breathe through a series of tubes attached to small openings on its body, which allow oxygen to pass to its cells. However, without a head it eventually dies from starvation!

Which Animal Removes Its Own Stomach to Feed ?

The common starfish (*Asterias rubens*) is not actually a fish but an echinoderm, which is closely related to species such as sea urchins. The common starfish can grow up to 3 feet (1 m) across and has five arms, which contain tiny suckers, and a central mouth underneath the upper body. However, there are some species that have as many as forty arms. Starfish mostly live in the Atlantic Ocean but are also found in the Mediterranean.

Starfish feed on clams, mussels, oysters, and worms. When they've found their food, such as a clam, they put their arms around it and grip it with their suckers, which gradually pull the victim's shell apart. The starfish then pushes its whole stomach out of its mouth and into the shell of its prey. Once inside, the stomach releases digestive juices and begins to slowly digest the clam. When it has finished its meal, it sucks its stomach back into its body through its mouth.

Starfish are extraordinary creatures in many ways. When they are attacked, some may lose an arm or two. However, this isn't a problem because they can simply regenerate new arms. Most species must have the central part of the body intact to be able to regenerate, but

starfish can regenerate new arms

a few can grow an entire new starfish from a single arm. Before this was known, fishermen would cut starfish into pieces thinking it would kill them, but the starfish grew into new ones, and so their population increased dramatically.

Why Do Hippos Use Their Tails to Fling Their Poop?

Most of the world's hippopotamuses are found in Africa and can weigh as much as 3.5 tons (3.2 mt). They spend most of their time in water, where they poop in copious amounts. The dung is important for the food chain, as it contains nutrients for many microorganisms, which are in turn eaten by fish.

Around the Nile, male hippopotamuses mark off their territorial boundaries by performing a disgusting ritual. They poop and spin their tails to distribute the excrement over the largest possible area on the riverbank. Hippos also urinate backward, probably for the same reason. At night, they leave their rivers and lakes to graze on grasslands. To ensure they can find their way back to the water, they mark their trail by leaving piles of dung.

hippos urinate backward

Which Frog Gives Birth through Its Mouth?

Frogs tend to lay a large number of eggs to maximize the odds of survival because there are many hazards between an egg's being fertilized and becoming a full-grown frog. However, some frogs have very unusual ways of helping to ensure that their offspring get the best possible start in life.

Male Darwin's frogs (*Rhinoderma darwinii*) attract the female frogs by singing to them. After this romantic court-ship, the female leaves the male to watch over the eggs. He gathers them up and swallows them, storing them in his vocal

the male swallows the eggs

sac. Here, the eggs develop into tiny frogs before being spat out into the world.

Another amazing frog was the Australian gastric brooding frog (*Rheobatrachus silus*), which sadly was only discovered just before it became extinct. This fascinating creature would lay its eggs in the water, where they would be fertilized by the male and then swallowed by the female. Inside the female's stomach, the eggs would develop into tadpoles before emerging five weeks later as baby froglets from the mother's mouth.

Can It Really Rain Frogs and Fish

Surprisingly, it is not only frogs and fish that have been reported to have fallen from the skies, but also showers of snails, maggots, worms, snakes, shellfish, and even lizards. There have been thousands of reports from all over the world of showers of either small fish or tiny frogs raining down. However, strangely, nobody has ever seen frogs, fish, or other animals being carried up into the skies. The only rational explanation for these bizarre rains is that tornados or water spouts are responsible. They tend to suck up whatever is in their path and, if the objects are light, take them into the storm clouds. A tornado can carry objects for several miles before eventually dropping them back to earth.

Notable documented events of strange rainfalls include:

- In A.D. 77, the Roman historian Pliny reported a shower of frogs that fell from the skies.
- In the fourth century, fish reportedly fell on a town in Greece for three whole days.
- In 1894, a bizarre shower fell on Bath, England, which was described as consisting of thousands of jellyfish the size of American quarters.
- During a storm in England in 1939, so many frogs fell from the skies that witnesses were afraid to walk around for fear of squashing them.
- In April, 1985, starfish fell into a yard in St. Cloud, Minnesota during a storm. They were believed to be from the Atlantic Ocean, over 1,000 miles away.
- Perhaps the most disgusting of all these strange events was that which occurred in

Bucharest, Romania, on July 25, 1872. On this day, the heat was stifling and the sky cloudless. At about nine o'clock, a small cloud appeared on the horizon, and a quarter of an hour afterward, to the horror of everybody, there was no rain, but small, fat, black worms or grubs covered most of the streets.

> fat, black **worms** covered most of the **streets**

Do Jackals Really Feed Their Offspring with Their Own Vomit?

The jackal, a doglike creature with a bushy tail, is found in many parts of Africa, the Middle East, and India. Jackals are members of the dog family, and their predators include leopards, hyenas, and eagles.

Jackals are scavengers that find and eat dead animals in order to survive. They will happily eat decomposing or diseased flesh riddled with maggots, even if it's been rotting for days. When lions and tigers are done with their kills, jackals will happily move in for the revolting leftovers.

Unlike many other animals, jackals mate for life, producing many offspring. After hunting for food, the parents swallow prey they have caught, and when they return to the den, the pups lick their faces until the parents throw up the softened food. This rotting, regurgitated mush is then fed to the young!

What Is Dangerous about the Silver Carp

In the 1990s, a type of fish called the silver carp first entered the Mississippi River after having escaped from a local fish farm following a series of floods. Since that time, the carp have steadily moved upriver, and now they outnumber local fish by ten to one and are spreading to other rivers in the area.

One unique danger posed by these fish is the

fact that they can leap out of the water; in fact, some have been known to jump 10 feet (3 m) in a single leap. It seems that one thing that makes them jump is the noise of boat engines—presumably because they think it is a predator chasing them—and this makes them especially dangerous from a human point of view, because it means they literally jump with fright at every passing boat. If only a handful of fish jumped at any one time, that would be dangerous enough (they can reach up to 100 pounds [45 kg] in weight—people have described being hit by a silver carp as like being hit by a bowling ball). However, they are known to leap in groups, with as many as two hundred leaping out of the water simultaneously, making them an even more serious menace.

There have been numerous reports of large jumping silver carp severely injuring boaters and water skiers. In June 2004, a woman water-skiing in Illinois was smacked in the head by a massive leaping carp and suffered a concussion.

Which Insect Is the Tarantula's Worst Enemy

The tarantula may seem like a fearsome predator, but it's no match for its worst enemy, a wasp called a tarantula hawk (*Pepsis heros*). The tarantula hawk wasp is one of the largest types in the world, with a wingspan that reaches 4 inches (10 cm) and a body length of up to 3 inches (7.5 cm). It is found worldwide and is typically metallic blue or black with brightly colored wings.

When the female wasp picks up the scent of a tarantula, she will hunt it down and then attack it. Strangely, the tarantula rarely attacks the wasp and becomes quite docile. Some experts think the wasp produces a pheromone—a chemical scent—that causes the tarantula to become stupefied. The wasp will then sting the spider, quickly paralyzing the arachnid with venom. The female wasp then lays an egg on the spider's motionless body and pushes it into a burrow. When the hungry baby wasp hatches, it starts eating right away. At first, it plunges its mouthparts into the spider's body and feeds on the spider's juices. But the larva grows quickly and soon begins eating solid foods—the spider's organs. All of this happens while the tarantula is still alive.

What Creatures Would Scare Me the Most

As is probably becoming clear, the natural world is full of disgusting, vile, nauseating creatures, but which is the creepiest to me? Here are the three contenders:

- The world's largest crab is the Japanese spider crab (*Macrocheira kaempferi*). Although its body measures only about 12 inches (30.5 cm), its outstretched leg span reaches more than 11.5 feet (3.5 m)! It can be found in the northern Pacific Ocean, where it lives in deep water and thankfully never surfaces. It is adapted to withstand great water pressure at depths of 3,300 feet (1,005 m) or more.

- The colossal squid (*Mesonychoteuthis hamiltoni*), which can grow to 39 feet (12 m) in length, could easily play a starring role in a horror film. It has huge, rotating hooks that grow from its suckers, an extremely large, sharp beak, and enormous bulging eyes, which are the largest eyes of any animal—the size of a dinner plate. In 2003, fishermen in the Ross Sea of Antarctica became the first people ever to see a colossal squid alive. It was feeding on fish caught on their fishing lines. It was almost 20 feet (6 m) long, about half its full, adult size.

the colossal **squid** can grow to **39 feet in length**

• Africa's goliath beetle (*Goliathus giganteus*) may win the prize. It is one of the biggest and heaviest insects in the world and can be found in tropical rain forests. They are as big as a human fist and measure about 6 inches (15 cm) long and 2 inches (5 cm) across, and their primary food source is feces. They are good fliers and make the sound of a low, helicopter-like whirr while flying. Sometimes African children like to tie their bodies onto string and watch them fly around in circles. Male goliath beetles have a horn-shaped structure on their heads, which they use to fight with other goliath beetles.

Why Do Herring Fart ?

Some fish, such as the male cod, are known to produce a kind of grunting or buzzing noise to attract females, but these noises are not really farts. The male cod makes this noise by vibrating an air-filled sac called a swim bladder, which lies beneath its backbone and is used to control the fish's buoyancy.

Another sea inhabitant that may seem to fart is the sand tiger shark, a ferocious-looking fish that has sharp teeth that protrude in all directions, even when the mouth is closed. The shark is denser than water and lacks a swim bladder, so it gulps air into its stomach at the surface of the water and then lets the air out in bursts to help itself sink deeper. This also allows the shark to float motionless in the water so it can seek prey. However, unlike human farts, these specialized emissions aren't produced by gas after eating.

One fish that does fart is the herring. They make a high-pitched noise while releasing bubbles from their anal duct. No other fish has been known to make noises from that area, or to produce such a high-pitched noise.

the sand tiger shark has sharp teeth that protrude in all directions

Biologists concluded that herring make farting sounds to let one another know where they are, and these noises are so high-pitched that only other herring are able to hear them. The team of scientists who researched this clearly had a sense of humor because they called this noise Fast Repetitive Tick, or FRT for short. While investigating if the sound was related to the herring's digestion, they found that the number of FRTs produced does not change when the fish are fed. Also, if the fish were starved, they still produced the sounds. One other theory was that the FRTs were produced out of fear, but this too was rejected. When herring were exposed to shark scent, there was again no noticeable increase in bubbles or sound.

The researchers eventually became convinced that the FRTs were most likely produced for the purpose of communication, for three reasons. First, they noticed that more FRTs were produced when the herring were in bigger shoals. Second, herring are noisy only at night, so they believe that rather than fumbling around in the dark, the fish can easily locate one another using their FRTs. Third, because only other herring can hear the FRTs, it is a safe way for them to communicate without alerting predators to their position.

Coming up...

an exploding king

6
Deadly Details

Can Medicine Be
Derived from Corpses ?

The dead have long been seen as potentially useful to the living, especially to help cure illness and
prolong lives. As far back as 1550 B.C., we have
records of human brains being cut up and used to
cure eye ailments, according to an ancient Egyptian medical text.

In ancient Rome, epileptic patients were often
prescribed several doses of human liver, which
was usually taken from a gladiator, because
gladiators were considered to be especially
strong and courageous. The ancient Roman philosopher Celsus wrote in his book *De Medicina*
that epileptics would be cured if they drank the
blood of a slain gladiator.

Through the ages, in many different cultures,
parts of dead bodies have been used as medici-
nal cures. For example, a cure for ulcers, goiters,
cysts, and diseases such as tuberculosis was to
touch a dead man's hand, preferably the hand of

someone who had died a premature death. Public executions attracted large crowds, and people gathered in hope that a hangman would let them touch the hand of the still-warm victim as he dangled from the rope. They would pay the hangman for the privilege. An enterprising executioner at Newgate Prison in London developed a similar, and profitable, sideline—he chopped off his victim's hands and sold them. Hangmen also made money from selling remedies made of herbs and human fat from their victims.

During the 1600s and 1700s, people in Denmark also believed that fresh blood would cure epilepsy. People flocked to public hangings and stood by the condemned, in the hope that they'd catch some blood in a cup. In the 1680s, human skulls were sold in London and people would grate them to a fine powder, which they would then consume. In 1721, the dispensatory of the Royal College of Physicians was recommending "three drams of human skull" to help epilepsy sufferers (that's about a teaspoon).

ground mummy powder was to be drunk as a tea

The incredibly well-preserved state of Egyptian mummies led European doctors from the Middle Ages onward to sell mummy parts as medication. In the 1100s, European doctors ground mummies into a powder, which they advised was to be drunk as a tea or used in a poultice for its numerous health benefits. It was prescribed for many ailments, including coughs, nausea, epilepsy, migraines, incontinence, gout, bruises, and even fractures! When mummy was in short supply, unscrupulous mummy suppliers quickly mummified the bodies of executed prisoners to be sold as ancient mummies.

King Charles II (1630–85) rubbed powder from Egyptian mummies onto his skin all over his body. He believed it would promote longevity and transmit ancient greatness.

Unsurprisingly, there is no evidence that eating any part of a mummy can actually help cure any ailment, so it's astonishing that its use continued until the seventeenth century. It fell out of favor mainly because of the problems associated with consuming it. French surgeon Ambrose Paré wrote that "not only does this wretched drug do no good, but it causes great pain to the stomach, gives foul-smelling breath, and brings on serious vomiting."

Where Can You Find a Bone Chapel?

If you fancy a gruesome family day out, why not visit the Chapel of Skulls in Czermna, Poland? As its name suggests, this church displays many bones; in fact, its chapel walls are lined with three thousand skulls and other bones. The ceiling is densely covered with hundreds of human skulls, each positioned above two crossed leg bones. There are more than 20,000 more skulls stored in the vaults. The chapel was the innovative idea of a local Czech parish priest, who created it in 1776 to act

its walls are lined with **three thousand** skulls and bones as a memorial to those who had lost their lives in the wars of the 1600s and 1700s. This popular attraction also contains the bones of some of the victims of the many cholera epidemics that plagued the area.

Another macabre chapel, called the Capela dos Ossos, or "Bone Chapel," can be found in Évora, Portugal. It was built in the fifteenth century by Franciscan monks, and is decorated with human bones and skulls from about five thousand bodies taken from local cemeteries. The bones are held together by cement and cover the walls and pillars of the chapel. The chapel also contains two dried-out, leathery corpses hanging from the ceiling, but their identities are unknown.

Beneath the city of Rome lie hundreds of tunnels that extend for miles and contain the buried remains of tens of thousands of people. Rows of tightly packed bones are piled from the floor to the ceiling and have remained there for almost two thousand years. In the second century, Christians started burying their dead underground, and the catacombs continued to function as cemeteries until the fifth century. The bones mostly belong to Christians, but the catacombs also house the bones of Jews and pagans. Burials of early Christians involved wrapping the body in a sheet or shroud and placing it into a niche cut out of the rock. The niche would then be sealed with tiles and fixed with mortar or a slab of marble, upon which the name of the deceased would sometimes be engraved. Some of the tunnels are open to the public for guided tours.

What Happened When William the Conqueror's Corpse Was Placed into His Tomb?

William the Conqueror (c. 1028–87) became King William I following his conquest of England at the Battle of Hastings. As a young adult, William was so fit that he could jump onto his horse when dressed in full armor. However, later in life he piled on the pounds and became grossly overweight. When

King Philip of France made some spiteful comments about William being too fat, William set fire to the small French town of Mantes in France. As the fire burned, his horse stepped on a hot cinder and slipped. This caused William to be thrown forward and fall onto the point of this saddle, therefore sustaining a nasty injury that caused internal bleeding. He died six weeks later.

As William was large and decomposition of his body caused it to swell, it became too big to fit inside the stone tomb. Legend has it that two soldiers had to stand on the body to push it in. In their desperation to cram it in, they jumped up and down on the body and broke its spine. The broken spine pierced the stomach, and because of the accumulation of gases, it exploded, splattering the poor soldiers with rotting flesh. The smell was so putrid that everyone, including priests, rushed out of the church to get some fresh air.

> decomposition of his body caused it **to swell**

Who Was the Woman Who Died Three Times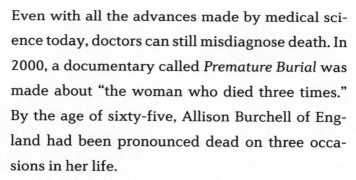

Even with all the advances made by medical science today, doctors can still misdiagnose death. In 2000, a documentary called *Premature Burial* was made about "the woman who died three times." By the age of sixty-five, Allison Burchell of England had been pronounced dead on three occasions in her life.

In 1952, when she was seventeen years old, she collapsed unconscious in a movie theater. She was rushed to the hospital, where she was pronounced dead. However, despite her body being paralyzed, she was able to see and hear clearly, and was aware of all the conversations being held by the nurses as they prepared her body and eventually took her to the mortuary. Thankfully, after about thirty minutes, she recovered and was then subjected to numerous tests, which revealed that she suffered from severe narcolepsy. This disorder has symptoms that include overwhelming drowsiness, sudden attacks of sleep, and cataplexy, which is a sudden loss of muscle control and can cause short-term paralysis. Narcolepsy can leave patients totally paralyzed, even though they are fully conscious and able to understand everything that's going on around them.

A few years later, Burchell suffered another attack and woke up in

she woke up in a mortuary, surrounded by dead bodies

a mortuary, surrounded by dead bodies. In the 1970s, she had moved to Australia and suffered a third attack. Again, she was pronounced dead, but her teenage son convinced hospital staff not to place her body in the airtight refrigeration unit. Burchell described the sensation: "You can see and hear everything going on around you, but there is no way to convey to anyone that you are not dead. It's the most terrifying thing imaginable." Thankfully, Burchell wasn't put into the refrigeration unit, and once again made a full recovery.

What Is a Waiting Mortuary?

During the seventeenth and eighteenth centuries, the rudimentary nature of medicine meant that there was a risk of people who were comatose or otherwise incapacitated being misdiagnosed as dead. Consequently, many people in Europe and America were terrified of being prematurely buried.

A German physician named Christoph Wilhelm Hufeland also took a great interest in premature burial, and believed that a body decaying was the only certain sign of death. He also thought that when a person died, they first entered into a state of deep unconsciousness, or death trance, which was not always fatal. A person could sometimes awaken from this state, which meant that there was a risk that they might be buried alive.

To solve this problem, in 1791 Hufeland built a "waiting mortuary" in Weimar, Germany, which consisted of a corpse chamber with eight beds. A fire was kept continually alight, and steam from boiling water was fed through underground pipes to the corpse chamber. This would make sure that any bodies that actually were dead would rot quickly, and thus prove they weren't alive. To help disguise the smell of rotting flesh, bouquets of flowers were placed around the beds.

any **bodies** that actually were dead would **rot** quickly

Additionally, there was an attendant employed to look out for signs of life, in case any of the bodies turned out to have merely been in a death trance. Each of the bodies had a bell attached to its fingers, which the attendant had to listen out for. According to reports, these bells would ring often, because the corpses would move and expand as they decomposed. Another gruesome and smelly job of the attendant was to clean up the mess associated with rotting corpses.

The waiting mortuaries turned out to have another benefit. As well as removing the risk of premature burial, the grieving family didn't have to keep the body in their home.

After the discovery of the heartbeat as a clear sign of life or death, the fear of being prematurely buried diminished. The last German waiting mortuaries were closed in the late 1890s.

What Is a Safety Coffin?

Waiting mortuaries were not the only innovations designed to protect people against the risk of premature burial. From the mid-1800s through the early 1900s, a number of coffin alarm devices were patented. In the 1850s, George Bateson made a lot of money from his very successful safety coffin, which was marketed as the Bateson's Life Revival Device. The device consisted of a bell with a rope that led through the lid of the coffin and was tied to the corpse's hands through the lid of the coffin.

coffin alarm devices were patented

If the corpse awakened, it could simply ring the bell for assistance. Queen Victoria awarded Bateson the Order of the British Empire for his services to the dead. During the Victorian age, his invention and other coffin bell alarms could be found in many of the new graves in cemeteries far and wide.

This book will make you itch!

Get ready to squirm!